EFFECTIVE TEACHING

THERE'S ONLY ONE WAY

by

Allene Mandry

Published by
R&E PUBLISHERS
P. O. Box 2008
Saratoga, California 95070

Typesetting by
Estella M. Krebs

Cover by
Kaye Graphics

Library of Congress Card Catalog Number
86-62494

I.S.B.N.
0-88247-762-5

Library of Congress Cataloging-in-Publication Data

Mandry, Allene, 1942–
    Effective teaching.

    1. Teaching.   2. Education--Aims and objectives.
3. Learning.   I. Title.
LB1025.2.M343   1987   371.1'02   86–62494
ISBN 0-88247-762-5

Dedicated to . . . .
Professors Sue Hawkins, Jean Wilson, and Bruce Frazee
. . . . excellent teachers!

80204

Table Of Contents

Preface

This book fulfills a desire that I have had for many years, a desire to share some of my ideas on how I think teaching should be done in order to be really effective. For the most part, the ideas presented in this book represent successful teaching methods that I have actually used in the classroom, in my graduate field experiences, and tutoring sessions. There was no research involved in writing the book, so it is not at all technical in nature. It is simply based on my experiences as a teacher. In addition, most of the ideas discussed do not pertain to any particular grade level. The book was written in this manner so that teachers of any grade level can adapt the ideas to fit the abilities and needs of their students. It is hoped that the material might inspire teachers to think of their own meaningful approaches to teaching as they read. For this purpose, a blank page is provided after each chapter so that the teacher can jot down ideas for future use. Furthermore, because teachers have little time for reading professional journals and materials related to their particular teaching fields, I have purposely kept this book brief and to the point.

I would hope that this book would be especially beneficial to beginning teachers. New teachers may be competent in their particular fields, but knowledge of a subject does not necessarily make a good teacher. Teachers must be able to convey that knowledge to the students, not only in terms which the students can understand, but also in ways which are meaningful to the students. It often takes years for a teacher to develop such successful teaching techniques in his particular field, and, unfortunately, teachers do not always share their ideas with other teachers nor do they have the opportunity to observe other teachers' classes. In fact, teachers are generally unaware of techniques or procedures used by other teachers. As a result, each teacher learns more or less from trial and error without the benefit of others' experiences. I want to share my ideas in hopes that they may help not only beginning teachers but teachers who may be looking for new ways to add meaning to their teaching.

Much of what takes place in today's classrooms is not real learning. Subject matter which is really learned need not be retaught year after year. Each new school year should provide a foundation for the next year's classes, but, instead, valuable time is wasted each year trying to teach students in a few weeks what they should have learned during the previous year. It is time that many teachers stop going through the motions of teaching and really teach. I believe that this can only be achieved by providing meaningful learning experiences for students, experiences which they can relate to real-life situations. Teachers must begin to realize that teaching is not having students read and answer questions day after day, but, instead, teaching is getting students involved in the learning process through participation, discovery, and discussion.

Before reading this book, I would like for you to consider the following questions and determine in your own mind if possibly you have just been going through the motions of teaching instead of providing really meaningful learning experiences for your students:

Do your lesson plans contain a variety of activities such as group work, classroom discussion, trips to the library, film-strips, and oral reading, or do students spend most of their time reading quietly from their texts and answering questions while you work at your desk?

Do your assignments require both critical and creative thinking skills, or do they basically require underlining and circling?

Do your tests contain a variety of questions, including both objective and discussion, or are they all multiple choice or matching for ease in grading?

Do your students know what to expect on tests, or are they surprised and bewildered when tests are passed out?

Do you promptly grade and return tests, as well as other papers, or do you wait a week or two when the material is no longer fresh on students' minds?

Do you stand at the classroom door at the beginning of each class to greet students, or are you busy working at your desk as students come in?

Do you talk in a normal pleasant tone of voice, or do you scream at your students and unnecessarily belittle those who cause problems?

Do you respect your students as individuals with different feelings and opinions, or do you expect them to conform to your ideas of what they should be?

Do you organize and have each day's activities planned, or do you often come to class as unprepared as some of your students?

Do you keep your students so busy that they have no opportunity to misbehave, or do you spend more time disciplining than teaching?

Do you thoroughly explain classroom and homework assignments, or do you give out work with little or no explanation?

Do you give students the opportunity to ask questions and discuss subject matter, or do you do all the talking in the class?

Do you look for ways to make learning meaningful, or do you really just go through the motions of teaching?

At this point, you're either very confident with your current approaches to teaching, or you're beginning to question the methods you've been using. Maybe you're even a bit angry at the author for posing such questions. Whatever the case, you, as a teacher, really need to evaluate your present teaching practices. Too often teachers get bogged down in a comfortable routine which they call teaching, a routine which uses the same lesson plans, worksheets, and tests year after year. Each day they go through the motions of teaching. Worksheets are distributed, completed, graded, and recorded, and the process is repeated the next day. Is it any wonder that so little meaning takes place in many of today's classrooms?

Today's teacher has to have a very special talent, a talent for taking the ordinary and making it something special and meaningful for the student. A teacher should approach a lesson by asking himself or herself, "How can I present today's lesson in a way that students will find the material meaningful?" This is an exciting and challenging goal for every teacher, and I guess that's what I loved most about teaching. How could I best reach my students? I didn't have to wait to see their grades either to see whether or not they understood a particular lesson or concept. The success of my approach was rerlected in their eyes and the expressions on their faces. There's a special sense of satisfaction when you know you're reached them all. This, indeed, is meaningful teaching.

1 When Is Teaching Not Teaching?

I must admit that the idea for this book was borne of frustration, a frustration stemming from hours spent each night explaining and clarifying material that was supposedly taught to and learned by my eleven-year-old daughter during the course of a typical day in middle school. Elementary school came too easy to her, and only occasionally did I question a teacher's method of presenting new material or concepts, and only once did I become angry enough to actually write a teaching suggestion at the bottom of a test which was sent home to be signed. I could easily see from my daughter's low test grade that she had no idea what the teacher had been talking about for the previous two weeks. My comments received an instant and quite lengthy reply from the teacher, who was naturally quite defensive. How dare a parent tell a teacher how to teach!

The key word here, of course, is teach. The problem is that teachers do not always teach. The word teach implies that someone is presenting material in a manner that someone else is understanding that material, and thus learning it. The two words teaching and learning go hand in hand. Teaching is not teaching unless there is learning.

1

A teacher can fill an entire hour with talk but fail to teach anything. This is unfortunate because many teachers feel that they have taught a lesson simply because they have gone through the motions of presenting the material. The low test grade that my daughter brought home surely indicated that she did not understand the material, but it may very well have been the teacher's grade on how well the material was taught. As a teacher, I was always overjoyed when all my students passed a test because I felt that they not only knew the material, but also that I had succeeded in teaching it to them. Those teachers who complain of students' low grades on a test may very well be indicting themselves as to the quality of their teaching. Perhaps it is time that teachers begin using tests as means of evaluating themselves as well as their students.

The point of the foregoing discussion is this. If teachers want to really teach and insure that learning is taking place, they must find a way to make the material meaningful to their students. In most cases, a student who does not understand an assignment or who does poorly on a test did not find the material meaningful to him at the time it was presented. The blame for not learning the material is placed on the student, though perhaps, the blame should be placed on the teacher for not adequately teaching the material.

The question then is, how does a teacher go about making subject matter meaningful to students? Surprisingly, all it takes is a little initiative. A teacher must simply think of ways in which the material being taught applies to the students and their lives. For example, last year my daughter was introduced to finding area in math. As a homework assignment, she had a worksheet filled with little figures of squares and rectangles in which she had to find the area in square inches or square feet. As usual, the teacher in me emerged as I watched from a distance. Out of curiosity, I asked her if she knew how to find the area of her room, and, just as I thought, she had no idea of how area applied to any real-life situation. To her, finding area was something done only to figures on a worksheet. Her teacher had obviously missed a wonderful opportunity in making the learning of area a really meaningful learning experience for her students. In presenting the idea of area, she could have had small groups of students find the areas of the classroom, the chalkboard, the bulletin board, or the windows in the classroom. Instead of finding the area of meaningless little squares and rectangles on a worksheet as homework, she could have asked students to measure and compare the various areas of rooms in their homes or perhaps determine the amount of carpeting that would be needed to carpet certain rooms. Students who have gone through the process of actually measuring a room and determining the square footage will not soon forget the formula for finding area because they have experienced a meaningful learning situation.

Opportunities for making learning meaningful abound in every area of the curriculum. The teacher must be alert to these opportunities even though they may present themselves at an inopportune time in the teaching schedule. Most teachers generally teach course material in the order it is presented in the text, but sometimes it may be necessary to revise those plans in order to take advantage of a meaningful learning experience. For example, this year, my daughter's social studies teacher taught a unit on latitude and longitude, an area which normally confuses students because it is of little consequence to them. My daughter's assignments consisted of such meaningless exercises as determining the coordinates of little ships drawn on a mimeographed globe and drawing in little dots at given coordinates on a map. Since September is the height of the hurricane season, an alert teacher could have coordinated this learning activity with the plotting of hurricanes and tropical storms. Students could have been asked to follow and plot the movement of hurricanes by listening to the coordinates given daily on television weather programs. This type of activity not only makes the learning of latitude and longitude more meaningful but also reinforces map skills. By using an approach such as this, students can relate subject matter to real-life situations and thus find meaning in what they are doing.

It is particularly important that science teachers be alert to meaningful learning opportunities. A newspaper or magazine article related to science can serve as an excellent topic of discussion for a class period or serve as an introduction to the day's lesson. This may mean a change in lesson plans for the day, but the learning which takes place will be well worth it. Even if the class is busy studying insects, something as important as an eclipse should take priority. A major earthquake or volcanic eruption in the news can serve as the basis of an excellent learning opportunity as can news concerning the space program, important medical breakthroughs, and environmental matters. Such discussions make students aware that science is a part of their lives and not just something found in the science text. In addition, these diversions from the subject matter at hand need not interfere with regular curriculum. In fact, such diversions can serve to stimulate interest in science as a whole. As a result, more learning actually takes place than would otherwise. It is equally important that the science teacher exercise some common sense in the timing of lessons. For example, it is somewhat ridiculous to study insects in the dead of winter when there are no insects to be found; yet, I actually know of a science teacher who assigned an insect collection during the month of November. Such an activity should have been planned for the very beginning of school while the weather was still warm and insects were abundant.

The key, therefore, to real teaching is constantly being on the lookout for meaningful learning opportunities. Teachers must be aware of what is going on in the world, what personalities and countries are in the news, and, perhaps, most important of all, what their students' interests are. A daily glance at the newspaper can provide a wealth of ideas for activities which will enhance almost any

4

subject. Keeping abreast of educational programs to be offered on television can provide additional resources for the classroom. I realize that it will not be possible to make every learning experience a meaningful one, but teachers should be alert to such opportunities and take advantage of them whenever possible. In the following chapters, I have attempted to bring together some ideas which I believe will aid in making learning a more meaningful experience, particularly for kindergarten, elementary, and middle school students and, in some cases, high school students. It should be pointed out, however, that the ideas discussed are not meant to supplement procedures already used in the classroom. Instead, such ideas should replace those procedures which are not achieving their goals. The activities I describe are simply new and exciting ways of presenting traditional subject matter, subject matter which otherwise may be of little consequence to the students.

2 Meaningful Learning Begins in Kindergarten

What better place to begin meaningful learning experiences than in kindergarten? Unfortunately, kindergarten children are often cast into a world of pencil-and-paper exercises which are not necessarily meaningful and for which many students are not cognitively ready.

Kindergarten is basically a time for developing concepts. Unfortunately, many kindergarten teachers begin the year with actual reading and math instruction, thus overlooking those concepts which are vital to an understanding of both the reading and math processes. Memorization of the alphabet does not mean that the child is ready to read. First must come the realization that the letters of the alphabet not only have sounds, but these letters and sounds go together to form words, which, in turn, stand for meaning. The same is true in math. The kindergarten child who can count to ten or twenty may have no idea what he is saying if he has not yet developed the concept of what number really means.

Kindergarten is generally a time of developing readiness, readiness for future reading instruction. It stands to reason that a child must know something about his world before he can read about it. In order that reading material be meaningful, the child must be able to relate the reading to something he knows. In other words, reading must be a meaningful experience. If a student cannot relate his reading to meaningful experiences, then reading becomes nothing more than word calling, a situation which may very well lead to reading difficulties.

How does the kindergarten teacher build concepts which will act as a basis for future meaningful reading instruction? The process begins by involving the students in as many learning experiences as possible. The key word, of course, is involve. Paper-and-pencil work will not accomplish this. Whenever possible, teachers should use concrete learning experiences so that students can relate their learning experiences to the world around them. Concrete learning activities involve letting students handle objects and materials and discuss their similarities and differences; they involve taking children on walks and field trips and letting them observe, touch, and explore the world around them; and they involve the teacher listening to children and transcribing their stories, feelings, and observations in the form of language experience charts. Concrete learning experiences certainly do not involve neat little rows of children sitting at their desks working quietly with pencil and paper.

Many schools use beautifully designed readiness kits or readiness workbooks as the basis of their kindergarten programs. These are quite impressive, but a closer look reveals that these programs and workbooks basically employ pictures, not concrete objects. Kindergarten children need to be working with the concrete world, a world which has real meaning for them.

At the kindergarten level, it is easy to transform an otherwise boring lesson into a meaningful learning experience. For example, consider a typical readiness lesson on visual discrimination which involves discrimination of the shapes square, circle, triangle, and rectangle. The teacher normally discusses these shapes and then gives the children a worksheet on which they must color circles red, triangles blue, squares green, and rectangles yellow. This is fine as an evaluative measure, but wouldn't the children be much more interested if they were introduced to each shape and asked to find examples of that shape in the classroom? For example, they may be surprised to find such rectangular things in the classroom as the chalkboard, the surface of a table, the surface of the teacher's desk, the panes in the windows, the classroom door, the bulletin board, and the chalkboard eraser. Not only is this meaningful learning, but it teaches the child to observe and to think. Another day's lesson might involve taking the children for a walk around the school grounds and having them pick out different geometric shapes in the environment. Consider the shapes in the sidewalk, the bricks on the school building, the flag, the tires on the school bus or the bicycles, the license plate on a car, and the lights in the traffic light at the corner. Students may even be surprised to find a triangle formed by the spokes in the rim of a bicycle tire. Such a walk not only develops visual discrimination but also aids in language development as students describe the many things they see. By careful questioning of students, the teacher can also reinforce other concepts such as use of colors, relationship words, and the concept of opposites. Such learning experiences can never be achieved through the use of worksheets.

Kindergarten offers many opportunities for interrelating the various areas of reading, math, science, art, and music, and thus further reinforcing skills and concepts. For example, an interesting art lesson could be developed using the different geometric forms previously discussed. The teacher might give each child an envelope containing an assortment of the four geometric shapes cut from construction paper. Using their imaginations, the students can form pictures with some or all of their geometric shapes and paste them on a large sheet of construction paper. For example, a circle and a triangle could form an ice cream cone, or a variety of small circles, squares, and triangles could form the face of a clown. Several students could get together and form a train with their shapes. This type of activity not only reinforces what the students have just studied but also gives them an opportunity to be creative, to develop motor skills, and to work cooperatively with others.

The lessons described are certainly more interesting and meaningful than coloring shapes on a workbook page, but they don't happen automatically. The teacher must always be alert to such opportunities for making learning a really meaningful experience. Prepared readiness kits and workbooks provide many ideas for developing readiness skills, but the teacher must consider whether or not the method presented is the most meaningful way to teach that particular skill or concept. Does the skill begin on a concrete level, one that will be meaningful to the child, or does it begin at the abstract level, a level for which students may not be ready?

3 English Doesn't Have To Be A Foreign Language

As a middle school English teacher, I quickly discovered that English was the subject usually most disliked among students. Obviously somewhere in the students' school experiences they had found English to be either too difficult or perhaps just plain boring and unrelated to their lives. However, my spirits were not dampened as I set out to make learning about our language an exciting experience. In fact, my goal as an English teacher was to have my students excited about coming to class each day. Now that may seem like an impossible dream to most English or language arts teachers, but it is possible. In fact, it is possible for any teacher who is willing to put forth a little extra effort, and, by extra effort, I do not mean buying extra materials or spending countless hours decorating bulletin boards or making eye-appealing charts. This extra effort simply involves thinking, thinking of ways which will make the material meaningful to the students.

Unfortunately, many students tend to view English as a foreign language instead of one which is a part of their daily lives. Somehow, learning about nouns, verbs, adjectives, and adverbs seems to

13

have little bearing upon their immediate existence. In fact, students often question the necessity of learning such things as the parts of speech, adjective and adverb clauses, and conjugation of verbs. Teachers are quick to respond to their queries with such answers as, "You'll need to know this for the next grade," or "It's in our books so we have to cover it." Consequently, students see no meaningful reason for really learning the material, and thus it is soon forgotten or perhaps never learned at all, and the teacher the following year goes through the same routine, teaching the same thing over and over again.

By using a meaningful approach to the teaching of English, the teacher does not have to defend the subject he or she will be teaching for the next nine or ten months. The students will know why they are studying about their language and why English is a necessary part of the curriculum. Everything we do, including school-related activities, takes on new meaning when we understand the reasoning behind it.

This all sounds very simple, but how does the teacher go about accomplishing this feat? First, let us look at the way an English class is usually conducted. I will use my daughter's sixth-grade English class as an example. Her first assignment during the first week of school was learning to identify nouns in sentences, and I dare say that this is the first area of study in every English class in almost every grade in almost every school. Since that time, her class has progressed to plurals and possessives, action and linking verbs, direct objects, and predicate nouns and predicate adjectives. This, of course, seems normal to the teacher who has taught this way from year to year. So what is wrong with this procedure? It makes sense to the teacher, but does it make sense to the students? Why do we learn these things? Why is it necessary to know what a noun is? Why must we know the difference between an action verb and a linking verb? These are questions that should be answered and then discussed before actually learning what a verb or a noun is.

Students need to know something about their language before studying the actual structure of it. However, few teachers spend time in this area, probably because such information is rarely included in the text, or perhaps they themselves have little background on the history of language. However, even a teacher who has little knowledge in this area can stimulate discussion by asking such questions as, "What is language? In what way did early man record his language? What is the origin of our writing system? Where did the English language originate? What are some words in our language which are borrowed from other languages?" The amount of detail and depth of discussion, of course, will depend on the grade level of the students. However, it is important that all students have some background knowledge as to the origin of the English language. This might include such things as some background information on the various language families, particularly the Indo-European family of languages and the Germanic branch; the origin of our alphabet and numeric system; contributions to English from other languages, and knowledge of such terms as slang, jargon, and dialect. Teachers will find that students are fascinated with the origin of words.

As the discussion progresses, the teacher will lead the students to the realization that rules are a necessary part of language. This can be accomplished through such questions as, "When was the first dictionary written? Why do you think dictionaries are necessary? What would happen to our writing if there were no dictionaries? What would happen to our language if there were no rules to go by? Why then do you think it is necessary to study English in school?" A final question might be, "Why is it necessary to use such terms as nouns, verbs, adjectives, and adverbs?"

Students should be aware that the purpose of English class is to teach them to communicate effectively, both in oral and written expression. Naturally, it is necessary that they know certain grammar

15

terms in order to understand the rules of grammar which refer to these terms. Students might be given the analogy of trying to explain to someone how to repair a car engine without knowing the names for any of the car parts. The same is true of English grammar. Telling a student that a particular verb in a sentence does not agree with the subject is of little consequence to the student if he does not understand the terms subject, verb, and agreement.

A teacher who follows the procedure described thus far will find that students are much more receptive to the teaching of grammar because they now have a reason for learning about nouns, verbs, and adjectives. The study of English grammar thus becomes a meaningful experience.

Once the actual study of grammar has begun, it is important that the students be given the opportunity to apply what they have learned. Unfortunately, most application is accomplished through dull little worksheets which only require that students underline or fill in the blanks. If the purpose of the English class is to teach students to speak and write effectively, then why do most assignments consist of underlining or filling in the blank with the correct word? Seldom are students asked to write original sentences or compositions using what they have learned. In fact, as I look back on my daughter's short school career of six years, I can only recall one composition that she was required to write, and that was last year in the fifth grade. This is indeed sad. Why do we require students to learn rules and terms if they are never required to use them? Certainly, real life does not involve daily underlining exercises. Then let us do something meaningful with what we have learned.

I believe that students should be required to write at every opportunity. For example, if the students are working on nouns, they should be required to write some original sentences and underline the nouns in each sentence. These sentences can be read aloud or put on the board by the students and discussed. Students of all ages

16

enjoy sharing their work with their peers, and surprisingly, students often learn more from each other than from the teacher. If the teacher wishes to give a worksheet in which underlining is required, she can liven it up by using the students' names in the sentences or making the sentences about things with which students are familiar, such as current movies, rock stars, television shows, or school activities.

Whenever possible, teachers should coordinate compositions with various areas of grammar which are currently being studied in class. For example, the study of adjectives and adverbs offers an excellent opportunity for incorporating descriptive writing. Suggestions for topics might include "A Haunted House," "The Ghost Town," "The Storm," "A Summer Day," or "The Beach." Students should be encouraged to use a variety of adjectives and adverbs. Also, it is never too early to introduce students to the use of the thesaurus as a means for adding some spice and variety to their writing. In addition, it is a wonderful vocabulary builder!

Teachers are often concerned that students do not always use complete sentences in their writing. They do okay with a list of sentences where they are required to tell whether the group of words is a sentence or a fragment. However, this type of exercise is futile when students revert to using fragments in their writing. To cure this problem, I devised a plan for making students more aware of what they were writing. Students were first required to write their favorite fairy tale in paragraph form. They were then asked to rewrite the story by numbering each sentence and writing it on a separate line. Students then read their sentences, analyzed each one individually, and decided whether their sentences were actually complete thoughts or only fragments. In this way, the students began to see what was meant by the terms complete and incomplete thoughts. The same process can be applied to any type of student paragraph. By requiring students to write each sentence on a separate line, they quickly learn to detect sentence fragments on their own. Punctuation mistakes also become more obvious when each sentence is treated individually. This process may be time-consuming, but it teaches students to analyze their own work.

If verb tenses are the subject of study, students can take a short paragraph of their own creation or the teacher's and write it once in the present, a second time in the past, and a third time in the future. This is certainly more meaningful than having students underline verbs in a sentence and write the tense of the verb.

One area of English that students often find boring is that of letter writing. Perhaps this is because they are required to write letters to imaginary people and address "pretend" envelopes which are drawn on notebook paper. As a result, the entire assignment becomes rather meaningless. Instead of writing letters to imaginary people, have the students write a real letter to a real person or place. For example, many magazines contain travel ads which offer free information or brochures. A library period could be arranged so that students might look through both current and back issues of magazines for ads which might interest them. This type of exercise is extremely rewarding particularly when students begin receiving replies to their letters. If magazines are unavailable, students can write to the chambers of commerce of the cities of their choice to ask for information.

Of course, English grammar encompasses more areas than those discussed here, but the purpose of this book is not to provide a complete course outline for teaching a particular subject. It is aimed, instead, at making the teacher aware that there are two ways to teach every subject: the traditional way and a meaningful way. The traditional way of teaching grammar is obviously lacking. If it weren't, then it wouldn't be necessary to re-teach the parts of speech every year from third through twelfth grades. In fact, entering college freshmen often do not know the basics of grammar. Could it be

that these students never found English grammar to be a meaningful part of their lives?

4 A Meaningful Approach to Creative Writing

In the last chapter I touched upon the area of creative writing, an area which is often neglected in our schools. Colleges continue to complain that entering freshmen cannot write a decent paragraph. I must admit that I, too, am appalled, if not embarrassed, by the quality of the simple thank-you notes received from graduating high school seniors for gifts I have sent. After twelve years of schooling, an eighteen-year-old should be able to compose a two or three line note that does not sound like something written by an elementary student.

Who is to blame for the lack of writing skills among our students? Of course, colleges blame the high schools; high schools blame the middle schools; middle schools blame the elementary schools. Unfortunately, very few teachers endeavor to teach creative writing skills. In fact, some teachers become so frustrated with trying to teach students to write that they give up completely. Others make no attempt at all. In fact, my daughter is now entering the second semester of sixth grade and has not been required to write a single paragraph in any class thus far during the school year. If this situation is representative of school in general, it is no wonder that students are lacking in writing skills.

Creative writing should begin in kindergarten. Of course, students at this age cannot write, but they can be creative. They can make up stories and dictate them to the teacher, who can then transcribe them. The same process can be used in the first and second grades or until the student is able to transcribe his own stories.

A student who is introduced to composition in kindergarten learns about the structure of sentences and paragraphs. By watching the teacher transcribe his stories, he learns that writing is done from left to right, paragraphs are indented, sentences begin with capital letters and end with puncutuation marks, and, most importantly of all, he learns that words stand for meaning. The words indentation, punctuation, and capitalization may not be in his vocabulary, but they are subtly being introduced to him.

Once the student is able to write his own compositions, he should be given as many opportunities as possible to express himself on paper. Three to five sentences might be sufficient in the early grades, but as students become accustomed to writing, the length of compositions will gradually increase on their own. The forms of compositions, of course, will vary depending on the grade level involved. Though the narrative is generally the style used by elementary students, middle school students should be introduced to descriptive and expository writing.

An excellent tool for developing writing skills is the journal. Each student keeps a spiral notebook in which he is required to write daily during the first five to ten minutes of class. The journal can be kept as a diary, or the teacher can give the students some lead sentences to help them get started. A lead sentence might be something like, "My favorite television show is _____. I enjoy it because. . . ," or "I (do, do not) believe there are people on other planets because. . . ." The journal can be checked periodically to see that students are writing in them. If the journal is for a grade, the students can designate the entry they would like graded. Besides developing writing skills, the journal serves as an excellent means for getting students quiet and busy as soon as they come to class. The first five to ten minutes of every class period can be designated as time to write in journals. Since this time is normally devoted to getting students quiet and checking roll, the activity does not take away from class time.

The journal, however, should not be the extent of students' writing experiences. Compositions should be assigned on a regular basis, perhaps weekly or bi-weekly. Writing dozens of compositions will not automatically make the student a better writer. The problem is that most students pay little, if any, attention to all the corrections and comments that the teacher has written on the graded paper. They generally look at the grade and toss the paper away. As a result, the same mistakes are repeated on the next composition. In order to correct this situation, I devised a mimeographed sheet entitled "Theme Sheet" which my seventh and eighth grade students were required to fill in after each composition was returned. This sheet, which contained room for approximately fifteen composition titles, listed various areas where students needed improvement in their writing. For example, I included such things as capitalization and punctuation mistakes, sentence fragments, no right-hand margin, changing verb tenses, comma blunders, subject-verb agreement, and poor transitional sentences. The types of mistakes listed will depend on the grade level of the student. A place for the grade and positive comments made by the teacher was also included. After each composition was graded and returned, each student was required to look over the comments on his paper and, in the appropriate place on the theme sheet, check off the places where he needed improvement. Compositions were then filed in the students' creative writing folders, along with their theme sheets, and returned to the teacher. Students were allowed access to the papers at all times. By using the method described, students not only are able to review the types of mistakes they are making, but they can also see if they have improved in a particular area.

The topics of compositions will vary depending on the subject matter being studied. Generally, compositions are related to stories the students have read in literature units, but, as suggested in the previous chapter, grammar can be incorporated and reinforced through creative writing. For example, the study of quotation marks can easily be incorporated into a narrative composition by requiring that the students use some conversation as a part of the composition. This type of exercise is more meaningful than inserting quotation marks and other punctuation marks in sentences on a prepared mimeographed exercise.

Students generally dislike any type of writing assignment, mainly because they really don't know where to begin. Their writing assignments are so infrequent that they have never developed any strategies for getting their ideas on paper. The average student, when given a composition to write, begins writing, decides he does not like what he has written, and starts over. The process is repeated at least a half dozen times by each student in the class, and thus the classroom trash can is usually full by the end of the class period. This situation can be avoided if students are given some type of procedure to follow. First, they should jot down ideas which they might want to include in their papers. The teacher might want to check over these ideas before students begin actual writing. This list of ideas will eventually be turned in with the final copy of the composition. Once students begin writing, they should be encouraged to cross out ideas which they do not like instead of starting over. In fact, I never allowed students to discard any of their ideas during the entire writing process. All scratch papers and rough drafts were stapled to the final copy and handed in. Students were also instructed to write on every other line on the rough copy so they would have space to make revisions. By following this simple procedure, students will find that writing can really be a meaningful learning experience.

If students are to graduate from high school knowing how to write effectively, all teachers, beginning at the kindergarten level, must accept some of the responsibility for developing writing skills. The job can't be left to those few English or language arts teachers who stress creative writing in their classes. Giving two or three writing assignments does little toward developing good writers. Thus, it becomes the responsibility of every teacher to expose the student to as many writing activities as possible. Isn't it time we got away from so many circling, underlining, and fill-in-the-blank activities which are so prevalent in today's classes?

5 "Copy, Define, and Learn by Friday"

Someone once remarked to me that one of my child's teachers was excellent because the students in her class were required to learn twenty-five words a week. The key word here is learn. Did the students actually learn those twenty-five words or did they memorize them just for the test on Friday? Did matching words with definitions on Friday's vocabulary test indicate that they knew the real meaning of those words? What would a test on the same words the following Monday show? How many of those words would they know a week later? Even if they still knew the meanings of the words, would these words become an active part of their vocabularies? Could the students actually use these words meaningfully in sentences? Can you see the point I'm trying to make? What a waste of time for both teacher and student and perhaps for the poor parent who has spent endless frustrating hours reviewing his or her child for Friday's ominous vocabulary test! I can relate to this so easily because I went through a year of these tests with my daughter. To begin with, what was the purpose of giving the twenty-five words? As far as I can see, the only purpose was another test score for the teacher's grade book. In this type of situation, the teacher does not teach anything, and certainly the students do not learn anything. This is not a meaningful learning experience.

How should a teacher go about teaching vocabulary in a meaningful way? First of all, presenting a list of words that isn't related to the subject matter at hand is a waste of time. I well remember my eighth-grade English teacher of some thirty years ago who would assign fifty words to be learned by the end of each six weeks. Not once during that time did he discuss or even go over the words in the list, nor were they included in any of the stories we read in class. Why give students words which they will not find in the context of their studies? Is it the teacher's desire to simply make the course difficult? A situation almost as bad is giving students a list of vocabulary words after a story or chapter has already been read. How often has a teacher given the assignment to read and then define the words at the end of the chapter? Doesn't it make more sense to introduce vocabulary prior to reading so students may better understand what they're reading?

Another important consideration is the number of words assigned to students. Of course, this will vary, depending on the level of the students involved. In the course of my teaching, I found that five to ten words were sufficient for middle school students. Isn't it more desirable that students really learn five words rather than memorize the definitions of twenty-five words and really learn none? My aim each week was to saturate the students with the five or so words they were to learn. The normal procedure for teaching vocabulary is for the teacher to list the words on the board and have the students copy and define them. Instead of just listing the words, why not introduce each new word through sentences in which students can initially figure out the meaning through context? Have them formulate their own definitions before actually looking up the word in the dictionary. Don't just stop at looking up the definitions.

Help the students to correctly pronounce the words. Discuss the etymology of the word and point out root words and affixes. Have the students think of antonyms and synonyms. Each day purposely use the word in class discussion and include the word in sentences on worksheets where possible. Give extra points to those students who bring in newspaper clippings or quotes containing their vocabulary words. Read these aloud at the beginning of class each day and then display them on the bulletin board. I guarantee satisfying results if this approach is used.

Teachers who are interested in having students build their vocabularies with really meaningful words should try this. At the beginning of each grading period, give each student a mimeographed sheet entitled "My Personal Vocabulary List." The purpose of this sheet is to have students list words that they encounter outside of school. A major source of these words will, of course, be television. In appropriate columns on the mimeographed sheet, the student will list his word, tell where he heard or saw it, define the word, and write a sentence using the word. The lists can be collected weekly to insure that students are filling out the form. When I used this procedure with my eighth-grade students, I collected the papers every Tuesday and returned them on Wednesday. A total of twenty points was possible each week, five each for the word, source, definition, and sentence. After five weeks, the points were totaled for a grade. Of course, more than one word a week can be required, and the points altered. However, it is my belief that building a vocabulary should be a pleasant and natural experience. If this type of learning experience becomes a chore, then the assignment's purpose is defeated.

Teachers should take advantage of every opportunity to build their students' vocabularies. A few minutes' digression from the subject at hand can make a term in social studies, science, or mathematics more meaningful to the students. For example, one of my frustrations mentioned in the first chapter was re-explaining the associative and commutative laws in mathematics. My explanation began by asking, not telling, my daughter the meaning of commute. Unfortunately, she did not know the meaning, so I gave her a sentence using the word commute and asked her to figure out the meaning using context. Her answer this time was "to change." She was then asked how this might apply to adding and multiplying numbers. This time she was able to explain the commutative law satisfactorily. A similar process was used to explain the associative law. "Oh, that's easy," she remarked when we finished. Yes, it is easy when terms become meaningful, when students can relate words or parts of words to things with which they are familiar. Even mathematics teachers can profit by taking a few minutes out to teach vocabulary in a meaningful way.

6 "A Word About Spelling"

Spelling lessons, like vocabulary lessons, often accomplish little in the way of actual learning. The usual procedure is for students to be assigned a list of words, perhaps on a Monday, and then tested over these words on Friday. Exercises, which accompany each spelling unit, are assigned to familiarize students with the new words to be learned. In addition, students may be required to write the words five times each and perhaps write a sentence with each word. This entire procedure sounds fairly normal and has probably been practiced for the last thirty years. However, doing a few spelling exercises or writing words five times each does not insure that students are really learning how to spell the words. True, they may make good grades on the spelling test for that week, but will they still know how to spell the words next week or next month?

Personally, I thoroughly disliked doing spelling exercises when I was in school, and I'm sure that most students feel the same way today. In fact, I found spelling lessons to be terribly boring both as a student and a teacher. Who really wants to do the same thing every week for thirty-six weeks?

I am not advocating that we do away with the spelling exercises found in the spelling texts. Many of them are very good. I do suggest, however, that teachers use some discretion as to which exercises are assigned. In many cases, certain exercises would accomplish more if they were done orally. As a teacher, I often found myself explaining an exercise to almost every student in the class on an individual basis. I suggest that, before assigning an exercise, the teacher should ascertain any problems or questions which might arise during the course of an assignment so as to save herself and the students time.

The exercise found in the spelling unit should not be the extent of the students' encounters with their spelling words. There are dozens of other activities which can either replace or supplement the spelling lesson and, in fact, actually add fun to the lesson and perhaps insure, too, that these words will not soon be forgotten.

Before the teacher assigns any type of exercise, students should be thoroughly familiar with the pronunciation and meaning or meanings of each word. This does not mean that students need to write out the dictionary pronunciation and the various definitions of each word. This type of assignment is generally a waste of time since students will already know the pronunciations and definitions of many of the words. In addition, students often have difficulty converting the information found in the dictionary to information which they can use in forming sentences. The teacher can readily ascertain the problem words by asking individual students to use the words in sentences or by asking individual students to spell the words orally. Spelling exercises can then be chosen which will be of most benefit to the students. With this type of approach, students realize that the teacher is attempting to meet their needs instead of merely assigning busy work.

Many spelling exercises are centered around phonics exercises. These, too, are fine if they truly help the students learn to spell the words. However, if students already know the spellings of most of the words, they should not be required to dwell on phonics. These exercises should be means to an end and not an end in themselves.

As an English teacher, I tried a variety of approaches to make spelling a fun as well as meaningful part of the course. I tried, as much as possible, to coordinate the spelling lesson with our grammar assignment for that week. Students were asked to determine the parts of speech of spelling words when used in their own original sentences. Often they were required to use a spelling word as several different parts of speech. Students were given extra credit for bringing in spelling words found in newspaper articles or other printed material. These words were then underlined and posted on the bulletin board. Often I created stories centered around that week's spelling words. The actual spelling words were left out, and students had to insert the correct word. For review, spelling words were sometimes scrambled on a mimeographed exercise, and students had to figure out the words. In mimeographed exercises and tests, spelling words were purposely included in the sentences so that by the time of the spelling test, students were thoroughly familiar with the words. The purpose, of course, of all these exercises was to saturate the students with their spelling words.

The students particularly enjoyed a game I devised for reviewing words the day before the spelling test. A stack of 4x6 cards was prepared containing several of each letter found in the alphabet. Each student was given two or three of these cards. I would then call out a word and those students holding the appropriate letters would come to the front of the room and arrange themselves in the correct order to spell the word. During the course of the review, cards were switched so that all students were given an opportunity to participate. Letters which are the same can also be given subscripts so that a word containing several of the same letter causes no problems. For example, if a word contains four e's, the student possessing an e with a subscript of one would be the first e in the word, and the student possessing an e with a subscript of two would represent the second e. The teacher can also sort through the letters before each review and remove those which may not be needed. He or she should also make sure that there are ample letters to spell all words in the list. The results of this approach are extremely beneficial, particularly for the child who has problems with spelling. If he fails to come to the front of the room when his letter is needed, he won't soon forget how to spell that particular word.

As for the actual spelling test, there are a variety of ways in which to make the test more interesting. The teacher can call out the word and have each student write a sentence using that word, or the teacher can dictate sentences containing one or more spelling words. In the first method, students can be given partial credit for at least using the word correctly.

Spelling tests can also be mimeographed. Words can be printed with particular letters left out. As the teacher calls out the words, students can fill in the needed letters. Students can also match spelling words to definitions or look for misspelled words within mimeographed sentences and paragraphs. The key word here is variety. Make the spelling test challenging, but fun.

It should be noted that spelling shouldn't be limited to the words in the spelling book. Student paragraphs in the English and language arts classes provide an excellent source for commonly misspelled words. It is wise for the teacher to keep a list of these words and occasionally discuss them with the students. In fact, an entire lesson can be planned around these words. This type of lesson is much more meaningful than a list of words which students may seldom or never use.

The emphasis on spelling is generally limited to the language arts or English class, but it should be a concern of all teachers. This doesn't mean that formal spelling lessons need to be conducted in each class, but each content area teacher can emphasize correct spelling in reports and in other written work. Students can also be responsible for learning the spellings of specialized vocabulary words such as those found in science and social studies. Imagine the impact that could be made if all teachers worked together in improving students' spelling!

7 Reading Classes Which Really Aren't

"Oh, you'll love teaching reading. There's really nothing to do. The students work out of these little skills books, mark their answers on a prepared answer sheet, grade their own papers, and record their scores. All you have to do is check to make sure they're doing their work every two or three weeks." This is what I was told by a reading teacher when I took over her seventh-grade reading classes in the middle of the year. Though I had never taught a reading class, I was appalled that this was all that these students had done for four months. Of course, I was none too popular with my new classes when I set out to group students according to reading abilities and plan special activities for groups and individuals who needed special help in an area. There were days when we read orally in groups or I read aloud to the entire class. Charts were posted at the beginning of each week so various groups knew what to do each day. Somehow I managed to divide my time among groups and individuals helping them with problem areas. The first few weeks were difficult, but students slowly began to appreciate my efforts, and I could see results.

Unfortunately, reading classes are probably among the most mishandled classes in school. Reading is not taught by requiring students to work silently in skills books or their readers. The teacher, not the text or the skills book, is the key element in the reading class.

If the teaching of reading is to be a meaningful experience for students, it should be a responsibility shared by all teachers. However, many content area teachers tend to feel that the teaching of reading is not their job. Students may do well in a particular skill in reading and fail to apply that same skill in another class. The problem is that many skills in reading class are taught from materials which are totally unrelated to anything the student is doing in school. Students apply their newly learned skills to worksheets torn or duplicated from a reading skills book instead of meaningful material. If students are learning how to use an index, then why not use the index in their social studies, science, or grammar book as an example? If they are learning the SQ3R study method, then why not try it on a real chapter in one of their texts? If getting the main idea is the skill, then let's look for main ideas in paragraphs from a social studies or science book. If guide words in a dictionary are being studied, then let's use a real dictionary, not an imaginary dictionary page on a worksheet. The real key to teaching reading skills is making students aware that these skills do apply to areas in their lives and not just to worksheets in the reading class. Therefore, the reading teacher should strive to make every skills activity a meaningful one.

Unfortunately, teachers often do more in a reading class to turn students off to reading than they do to turn students on to reading. Students come to reading class expecting to read, but they suddenly find themselves doing dozens of little worksheets over the same skill day after day, week after week. If it's obvious that a student knows a particular skill, then why drill him to the point of boredom? Go on to something else. Even if a student is having difficulty with a skill, it is sometimes wiser to come back to the area later. Perhaps the best example of overdrilling students in reading is the area of phonics. The purpose of phonics is to help students learn to read by providing them with an important word attack skill. Many students do need to work on phonics if they are having problems with reading, but many teachers insist on phonics drills when it is obvious that a student is an excellent reader. Too much time in school is wasted on unnecessary drill and what many teachers and students term "busy work."

The attitude of the reading teacher plays an important part in the reading class. It is she who must instill in students a desire to read. If she is not excited about reading and books, then how can she expect her students to be so? She must surround her students with interesting reading materials. Shelves and shelves of readers and skills workbooks are not likely to foster positive attitudes toward reading, particularly among students who have reading difficulties. Reading materials in an idea reading classroom should include racks of paperbacks, magazines, comic books, encyclopedias, and news-papers. Newspapers, in particular, are an excellent source of skills materials for upper elementary, middle school, and high school students. Teachers will find that high school students respond positively to newspapers, whereas they may consider readers and skills materials to be of an elementary level. To them, the newspaper is a symbol of the adult world.

The exciting thing about using the newspaper is that students are learning about their world while they are developing valuable reading and thinking skills. Articles can be cut out, titles removed, and students asked to develop their own headlines, thus practicing skills in finding the main idea. Actual headlines can then be compared with ones written by the students. Comic strip frames can be individually clipped and students asked to put them in the correct order, thus practicing sequencing skills. Comic captions can be removed and students asked to write their own captions, thus practicing inferencing skills. Newspaper articles are excellent for getting students to think in terms of cause and effect relationships. They are also excellent sources for developing skills in recognizing fact and opinion as well as studying propaganda techniques. The possibilities are endless, but, of course, the difficulty of the skill will depend on the reading ability of the student involved. At any rate, the newspaper offers an interesting alternative to reading texts and skills worksheets.

The reading class doesn't have to contain expensive equipment or fancy reading kits in order for meaningful learning experiences to take place. With a little thinking and planning on the part of the teacher, almost any type of reading material can serve a useful purpose. Consider the many possibilities of the telephone directory and the yellow pages or even the weekly television guide. What about road maps, product labels, recipes, and directions found on various containers? If students are going to be able to function in today's world, they must have the reading skills to use all these things effectively.

8 Meaningful Math Experiences

Though mathematics is not my teaching field, I have had some experiences as a math tutor and have worked with students during my graduate studies. As a parent, I have spent many hours over the years helping my own child with her homework, and it is mainly through this experience that I have developed my own ideas as to how math should be taught.

Like any other subject, there is a meaningful way to teach math. The basic purpose of math is to teach the student the skills necessary to getting along in life. The problem is that students often see little relationship between what they learn in the math class and their present lives. The goal of the teacher, therefore, should be to help students not only learn the skills but also to show them how these skills apply to real life. Only then will the learning of math become meaningful to the student.

One of the first math experiences for children is that of counting. Kindergarten students proudly display their counting ability by counting to ten, twenty, fifty, or perhaps a hundred. Can they really count, or is it just memorization of meaningless words?

Can they count the number of buttons on their shirts, chairs in the room, or tiles on the floor? Unfortunately, students are often introduced to counting in school by giving them worksheets on which they must underline or circle the proper number of bunnies, kittens, or apples. Before exposing children to paper-and-pencil exercises, teachers should relate counting to the students' lives, to things that are important to them. How many crayons are in the box? How many cookies are in your lunch box? How many children are sitting at your table? It is important, too, that the teacher reinforces the concept of number by using numbers at every opportunity.

In the early grades, students learn to add and subtract, but here again most work is done in terms of paper-and-pencil exercises. Of course, it is essential that students learn the basic math facts of addition and subtraction, but sometimes these facts are meaningless as far as the students are concerned. It is important that the teacher initially present these math facts concretely. Let the students actually see that $7 + 4 = 11$ by using real objects such as pencils, paper clips, or pennies. Let the students handle the manipulatives and arrange them. Let them discover various sets of numbers which equal eleven such as $2 + 9$, $3 + 8$, $4 + 7$, and $5 + 6$. Students can be divided into groups and given manipulatives with which to work. For example, one group can be asked to discover sets of numbers which add up to twelve while another group may work on sets of numbers which add up to thirteen. Students can prepare flash cards for the class on specially cut cards showing what they have learned in their groups. This is certainly more meaningful than simply memorizing a sheet of meaningless math facts.

Manipulatives can play an important part in helping students learn their multiplication tables. Consider the student who knows that $2 \times 9 = 18$ but does not realize that 9×2 also equals 18. Though obvious to the teacher, the student may have difficulty in comprehending such a simple operation. To help students see that both

2 x 9 and 9 x 2 produce 18, simply lay out two rows of nine pennies or other objects on a piece of construction paper. Have one student count the pennies and confirm that 2 x 9 is 18. Then slowly rotate the paper so that there are nine rows of two pennies. Have another student confirm that there are still eighteen pennies. This simple procedure not only facilitates the learning of multiplication but also again makes learning a meaningful process.

A major source of difficulty for students at all levels is the word problem. This almost seems paradoxical in that word problems are attempts to get the student involved in actually applying his knowledge of math to real problems. He certainly won't go through life doing worksheets. If the student can't apply his math knowledge, then valuable time has been wasted. Perhaps the problem lies in the types of word problems that are found in most textbooks. Students generally find them uninteresting and totally unrelated to their lives. Indeed, who is interested in working a problem just to discover how many apples or oranges are left in Susie's basket? If this is indicative of the types of word problems found in the math text, then perhaps the teacher should make up some problems which involve things that are of interest to students and thus make the assignment a meaningful one. To make the problems interesting, actual names of places, people, and products can be used in situations students encounter in their lives. Students can even be asked to make up word problems related to their own experiences. The teacher can then take some of the better problems and duplicate them for the entire class to solve. Of course, the assignment will be even more interesting if the names of students who made up the problems are included. Students' word problems can also be discussed and analyzed by the class to determine whether or not there is enough information revealed in each problem in order to solve it.

An area of math which has particularly concerned me has been that of money and word problems dealing with money. My daughter was introduced to money in the second grade, and I can remember the many problems that she had in learning such things as how many pennies in a nickel, nickels in a quarter, and quarters in a dollar. Perhaps the cause of the problem was really mine for not teaching her the value of the dollar, but I really question whether most seven-year-olds know much about money. At any rate, if money concepts are going to be taught in the early grades, then experiences with money must be meaningful. First of all, learning about money from pictures of money is certainly a meaningless experience. Play money is helpful, but real money should be used, particularly in the earlier grades. Students can work in small groups with a specified amount of money as the teacher poses questions. To make the lesson even more meaningful, the teacher can bring in items such as popular candy bars or their wrappers, empty soft drink cans, and various school supplies and let the students decide which denominations would be necessary to purchase specific items. Depending on the grade and the difficulty involved, many kinds of learning experiences can be planned around this type of activity.

Elementary students often have difficulties with the concept of time. Time means little to young children, so studying little pictures of clocks in a math book accomplishes little. Teaching students how to tell time should not be reserved for a chapter in the math book. Teachers who are planning to teach time should begin the year by referring to time at every opportunity. Instead of telling students that it is time for art, recess, or lunch, the teacher should actually point to the clock and stress the time. "Children, it is now 10:15 and we will have recess for 15 minutes." He or she should also tell students how long they will spend on each activity so that they begin to gain some idea as to how long ten minutes, thirty minutes, or an hour may be. Teachers will find that the learning processes described introduce time concepts both subtly and meaningfully, and when it does come time to study these areas formally, the material will not be totally new to the students.

Students generally have some difficulty with the area of measurement. Learning that two pints equal a quart or eight ounces equal a cup means little to the elementary student who never has any occasion to use such measurements. Even less meaningful to students is the metric system. To them, these are only numbers and terms to be memorized and soon forgotten. Here again, teachers need to relate the information to the students' lives. For example, when working with measurements of volume, students should work with containers such as measuring cups, empty milk cartons of varying sizes, and soft drink cans and bottles. Using water, small groups can experiment with the containers and solve problems that the teacher poses. An interesting project might be preparing simple recipes which require no cooking but do require the use of measuring devices.

Similar procedures to those used in measuring volume can be used in working with linear measurements. Students can be grouped in pairs and asked to measure each other's height in inches and centimeters or to the nearest foot, meter, or yard. Measurements can be taken of the classroom, furniture in the classroom, and various school supplies. Too often, students only work with pictures in the text which, in most cases, are not life-sized. Therefore, students find it difficult to visualize such measurements as two yards, ten meters, or twenty feet.

In working with measurements of weight, students should be given the opportunity to weigh a variety of objects both in the U.S. Standard and the metric system. The possibilities for problem solving are infinite, but, of course, the complexity will vary with the grade level. Students can perform such simple operations as weighing paper clips and pencils, or various edible products such as candy, packaged foods, and canned drinks can be weighed to see if the weight shown is accurate. Students can also look for products in their homes which have weights listed in milligrams, grams, ounces, or pounds.

A variety of word problems can be centered around all of the measuring activities discussed. Students can determine whether it is more economical to buy their favorite soft drinks by the quart or the can. Is it more economical to buy certain products in the giant size or regular size? Is it less costly to buy some fruits by the sack or by the pound? Newspapers with grocery ads can be brought to class, thus teaching students to comparison shop. The possibilities are endless.

Graphing is an area in math which often has little meaning to students. Math books generally contain graphing activities that deal with such information as U. S. wheat production in certain years or populations of major U. S. cities. Why not have the students graph information which is of interest to them? Students can be divided into groups and each group given a specific project such as graphing the number of students who have birthdays in each of the twelve months or taking a poll of fast food restaurants and graphing the students' choices. Groups may even want to determine their own projects. Final graphs of all projects can be drawn on poster board and displayed for the entire class to see.

Fractions are a source of difficulty for many students. Fractions are generally introduced in the math book through pictures of circles or squares divided in halves, thirds, or fourths. Perhaps a more meaningful way of introducing fractions would be to use things with which students are familiar, such as an apple, a candy bar, a sandwich, or a soft drink. Using these objects, the teacher can demonstrate various fractions. When students fully understand the concept of fractions, they can progress to using large construction paper circles which have been divided into halves, thirds, fourths, eighths, or sixteenths or whatever the teacher desires. Each full circle should be the same size but of a different color so that students can locate them quickly. These circles can be kept from year to year in large envelopes, so it will not be necessary to make new sets each year. Students can work independently or in groups on various activities. These circles are excellent for studying simple problems of addition, subtraction, multiplication, and division of fractions. For example, students could place one-fourth and one-fourth together and discover that these two-fourths cover the same amount of area as one-half of one of the other circles. By working in groups, students can pool their envelopes of circles and have sufficient circles to work many types of problems involving fractions. Once students understand fractions at the concrete level, they can move easily to the abstract world of problems on a page in a math book.

One final area deserves some attention. However, this particular area is not one which is concerned with the teaching of any particular math concept. It is instead a procedure which has long puzzled both students and parents. Why is it necessary for a student to do fifty or a hundred problems of one type when it is obvious that he understands the process after ten or fifteen problems? A great deal of time is wasted in the classroom and at home from such senseless assignments. This time could surely be used for more worthwhile activities.

Though most of the areas of difficulty discussed concern elementary and middle-school students, many of these ideas could be utilized at the high school level. Students of all ages more easily understand subject matter which is presented in a meaningful way. Math teachers should always be alert to finding new and more meaningful ways of presenting concepts. The teacher must not let the textbook become the extent of learning in the math class, but, instead, he should only let it serve as a basic guide upon which learning experiences will be built. If students are to see that mathematics is really applicable to their lives, the teacher must make use of the home and school environment by drawing from these areas examples and problems which are a meaningful part of the students' lives.

9 Meaningful Library Experiences

I felt that somewhere in this book there should be at least a short chapter devoted to the use, or lack of use, of the library. As a student in elementary, middle, and high school, my experiences with the library were rather disappointing, if not frightening at times. The librarian regarded the library as her private domain, a place where one must not utter a word nor stay more than five minutes. Those who entered her doors must find a book and get out.

During my first years of teaching, I was surprised to find that the situation had not changed very much. I had my ideas about how the library should be used, and, of course, the librarian had hers. This situation was certainly disappointing to me, for how could a teacher possibly develop in her students a familiarity with, as well as an appreciation for, the library?

Fortunately, not all librarians are like the ones I have encountered. However, if the situation does exist, I suggest that the teacher speak to the principal and get the situation corrected. After all, the library is there for the benefit of the students and not the librarian.

One might be surprised at how many students never go to the school library unless the teacher takes the entire class, and then, of course, the reluctant student has little choice. Those students who do not utilize the library either have had unpleasant experiences there in the past or have no idea how to find what they are looking for. To them, using the library has become a chore instead of a meaningful learning experience.

It is essential that teachers take their students to the library as often as possible. A trip once or twice a year is of little value to the students. Then, too, the teacher should not feel that every trip must have an assignment attached to it. Because students rarely have time to just browse in the library, library periods should be scheduled in which the students are given time to explore the library on their own. The teacher can mingle among the students answering any questions that they might have. Many students will be surprised to find their favorite magazines, current newspapers, and paperback racks.

Generally, it is the English, language arts, or reading teacher who introduces students to the library. However, it is important that all subject matter teachers set up time to visit the library. The Dewey Decimal System becomes more meaningful to students when specific teachers point out areas where students can find additional materials in their particular subject area. This not only includes books which can be checked out but also magazines and reference materials. Even art and music teachers can profit from trips to the library. All teachers are responsible for seeing that students know how to use the library. The responsibility should not always be placed on the English teacher.

Of course, as the need arises, there should be special library periods set up for specific purposes such as using the card catalogue, the Reader's Guide, and reference materials. Too often these areas are covered in the classroom through the use of worksheets instead of first-hand experience.

Once students are familiar with the set-up of the library, the next step is to get them to use it on their own and not just when there is a book to be read for a book report. The librarian once remarked to me that she always knew what we had been discussing and reading about in my classes because there was a sudden interest in a particular subject in the library. How does a teacher go about stimulating interest of this sort in the library? The day before introducing a new area of study, the teacher simply goes to the school library and checks out several books which he or she feels will interest the students. Then, on the day of that particular lesson, display them at the front of the room, perhaps along the chalkboard tray. In English or reading, for example, the teacher might want to choose several books by an author being discussed in class. She might briefly discuss the titles and tell where they can be found in the library. This approach serves as an excellent introduction to that day's lesson. If the lesson is about a particular type of story such as mystery, biography, fantasy, or mythology, then samples of these books can be displayed. If the topic is sports, then the teacher might want to bring in a variety of books, some fiction, some biography, and perhaps some in the how-to category. The general idea is to let students know that these books are available in their library.

Most school libraries contain a variety of beautifully illustrated books on science and social studies. Science and social studies teachers who do not take advantage of these books are missing a great opportunity to stimulate interest, not only in their particular subject area, but also in the library. Consider the social studies teacher who is teaching a unit on Greece. No doubt there are numerous books in the library, not only on the geography of Greece, but on Greek history, travel in Greece, and Greek mythology. The science teacher who is presenting a unit on rocks should not miss the opportunity to stimulate student interest in volcanoes, fossils, and even dinosaurs by displaying a few of these books on the chalkboard. Books on these topics are usually attractively illustrated and thus appealing to students. One of the greatest joys to me as a teacher was to see a student with a book related to something we had talked about in class. To me, this is meaningful teaching.

If all teachers were to encourage an interest in the library by using the procedures described, there certainly would be little need for students to memorize the Dewey Decimal System. I say memorize for that is usually what students do. When students use the library regularly, they know exactly where to go to find certain kinds of materials. I can think of nothing more boring than sitting in a language arts class learning about the library, the card catalogue, and the Dewey Decimal System from a mimeographed sheet rather than first-hand experience. Of course, some classroom work is necessary, but the most meaningful time will be spent in the library itself.

Another interesting way to stimulate interest in the library is to write a rather difficult trivia question on the board each day. To discourage discussion of the answer among students, the teacher can reward a specified number of students, such as the first five students with the correct answer, with extra points or privileges. Another possibility is having students drop their answers in a box for a drawing at the end of the day or week. Each subject area teacher can find trivia questions which pertain to his subject area so as to further knowledge of that subject.

Another possibility, similar to that of the trivia idea, is to start the week with a rather general clue such as "I was a President of the United States who was born during the nineteenth century." Notice that this clue is so general that others are necessary to discover the answer. Each day the teacher will add a clue which will lead the students closer to the answer. On Tuesday, the teacher might give the clue, "My father was a Presbyterian minister." The third clue might be, "I was the only President to have a child born in the White House." The final clue should be very easy, for by then many students should have come up with the answer. A final clue might be, "There is a city in Ohio which bears my last name. It was named after my uncle." Of course, the answer is Grover Cleveland. Students should be allowed only one guess, to eliminate "wild" guesses on the first two days. Students can submit their answers on specially prepared slips of paper, which not only provide a place for the student's name and answer but also a place for the time and date when the answer was submitted. The teacher can enter this information to insure fairness in the contest.

When making up the five questions for the week, teachers should not just rely on information found in encyclopedias. He or she should also try to get students involved in using the dictionary, the card catalogue, magazines, and the atlases. The answer to a trivia question might even be a character or place in a story. The possibilities for questions are endless.

The library should be an integral part of classroom activity. It not only offers a valuable addition to the information found in the student text, but it provides opportunities for the student to be resourceful, to find answers for himself, and to expand his thinking skills. Don't let this valuable resource go to waste!

10 Making Social Studies Come Alive to Students

In this chapter I have combined the areas of geography and history under the broader heading of social studies. I debated for some time as to whether I should write a separate chapter on each area or combine them in one chapter. Both areas are distinctly different in the type of subject matter, but both require similar teaching strategies because of the tremendous amount of material involved in a single text. Students are suddenly faced with a multitude of facts, dates, maps, charts, and specialized vocabulary terms. In addition, they are introduced to people and places which hardly seem real to them. Students may not be equipped with the necessary reading and study skills needed to handle the type of material found in the social studies text. Indeed, both teachers and students are faced with a real challenge.

I must admit that I have always envied teachers of social studies. As an English teacher, I had to look for ways to excite my students about the subject matter in the English text, but for the social studies teacher, the excitement is already built in. What a wonderful opportunity to learn about people and places of both today and long ago! It would seem that today's beautifully illustrated geography and history texts would stimulate the interests of every student, but, unfortunately, this is not always the case. For many students, the study of geography becomes nothing more than meaningless memorization of states and countries and their capitals. For younger children, and perhaps older ones, too, there is little realization that the places read about really do exist, that there are children in other countries, just like them, who are going to school and learning perhaps about a far away country called the United States, its capital, political divisions, products, and terrain. Even more challenging is the task of making history a meaningful experience for students. Elementary and middle-school students and, indeed, many high school students see little use in studying about the past. They look upon history almost as a fairy tale or a story, not as a series of events which actually happened to real people, people who were just like them in many ways, people who experienced the same emotions as they do, and people who were perhaps students just like them who were required to also study history in school. It's difficult for them to imagine George Washington or Abraham Lincoln or even Julius Caesar as children or teenagers, but they were at one time. Once teachers can get their students to think of history as real events happening to real people, then it begins to take on a new meaning.

The secret, therefore, to teaching social studies is to make the material in the text come alive to the students. They are studying about real people and real places! The teacher should seize every opportunity to point out and discuss places on the map and globe, both in the geography class and the history class. She also has at her disposal a wealth of material in the newspapers, television, and movies. She should not be reluctant to discuss a place mentioned in the news headlines or on television simply because it isn't scheduled to be covered until next week or next semester. If Central America is in the news, take a few minutes to discuss its location and its importance to the United States even though that day's lesson may be on France or Italy. Students should be called on to locate the particular area under discussion on the map or globe. An alert teacher can use this learning experience as an opportunity to reinforce learning which has already taken place: Where is the Equator? Central America is located between what latitudes and longitudes? What oceans border Central America? On what continent is Central America located? What countries make up Central America? Where is Central America in relation to the country we are now studying? How are these places alike? How are they different? The possibilities for questions are endless. However, in order for meaningful learning to take place, the teacher must remember one important thing. He must let the students answer the questions and do the locating of places on the map. This is a learning experience for them, so it is important that they be active participants in the process.

I would like to stress the importance of maps in the classroom. Of course, maps are a must in the social studies classroom, but just having them there isn't doing the job. They should be used at every opportunity to reinforce material being studied. They shouldn't be equipment issued to the teacher at the beginning of the year and returned unused at the end of the year. Too, they shouldn't be pulled down or unrolled just for the day's lesson but should be available to students at all times. Teachers might be surprised to find that students are fascinated by maps. I discovered this quite accidentally when I taught history for a year. Prior to class, I had pulled the map down to cover some information I had written on the chalkboard for use later in the class. Before class started, students began crowding around the map locating various places they had been or were going to visit in the future. I was amazed at their interest, so I obtained several road maps of my state and the United States and placed them around the room so that all students might have the opportunity to look at them when they had some free time.

When discussing a new place such as a city, state, or country, or referring to the site of an event in history, it is important that the teacher first ask if any of the students in the class have been to that place or know anything about it. Information from peers is often more meaningful than information provided by the teacher. Some students whose parents are in the military may have traveled extensively and may be able to provide valuable information on an area. Students may also be acquainted with areas through movies, books, magazines, and television. When a teacher introduces a new area of study, he or she should also try to bring in some little tidbit of information which will not only arouse the interest of the students but will make that particular place more meaningful to the students. For example, how many students will soon forget Romania when you remind them that Transylvania, famed for its tales of Dracula, is located in the central part of that country? Romania is also famous for its Olympic women gymnasts, so the teacher might want to use this information to initiate a discussion on the country. Every city, state, or country has something interesting or unusual about it which a teacher can use to heighten interest in the classroom. There are Scotland and the Lochness monster, Egypt and King Tut's tomb, Los Angeles and the La Brea Tar Pits, Australia and its sharks, the Amazon and piranhas, and the Himalayas and the abominable snowman. These topics will surely capture the interests of students at all grade levels. Sometimes it might take a little extra research on the part of the teacher to find somthing particularly interesting about a place, but the effort is certainly worthwhile if it helps to stimulate class interest in an area being studied.

Of course, social studies is not limited to locating places on a map. There is also the matter of a multitude of new vocabulary terms which students will encounter in their reading. As suggested in the chapter on vocabulary, do not overload students with more

62

words than necessary. Choose those words which are necessary to understanding the material in the chapter and remember, these words should be introduced prior to reading the chapter and not after. Defining words after the chapter is read serves little purpose. Try to make vocabulary come alive for the students. Talk about the words, ask for and give examples, and where possible, have students illustrate terms such as peninsula, plateau, tributary, levee, latitude, and longitude. Have students bring in clippings from newspapers which contain vocabulary words. In other words, saturate your students with each new set of vocabulary terms.

Once the actual reading of the social studies text is begun, students may no doubt be overwhelmed by the number of dates, facts, events, and people found within a single reading assignment, particularly in the history text. The teacher must take the responsibility for helping students develop some strategies for handling the material. Having students read a chapter and answer the questions at the end of that chapter does not insure that students are learning the material. Neither is it a very meaningful approach to teaching history, nor is it helping students develop any study strategies. SQ3R, of course, is an excellent study method, but it is only effective if it is used consistently by both students and teachers. I was overjoyed this year when my daughter was introduced to this method during the first six weeks of her social studies class. However, the students only used this method on one chapter and were then tested over the method itself, thus defeating the whole purpose of learning the method. Using SQ3R on one chapter certainly does not insure that students will use the method on their own.

Perhaps the biggest problem in history is simply getting students to read the material in the text. Many teachers try to solve the problem by assigning sheets of fill-in-the-blank statements taken word for word from the text, often with page numbers provided for ease in finding the answers. However, this procedure usually doesn't work because students search for sentences containing the correct answers instead of reading every sentence on the page. As a result, little is accomplished by the assignment, for instead of getting an overview of history, students come away from the assignment with a series of disconnected facts.

When evaluating any approach to teaching history, teachers should consider the following questions: Does this approach help students to develop their own learning strategies? Are students learning to think for themselves? Are students getting an overview of the material, or are they learning dozens of meaningless, disconnected facts?

At one time, I taught in a history department where all teachers used departmentalized worksheets which accompanied each chapter in the text. Students generally worked on the worksheets in class for two or three days, after which papers were exchanged and graded by the students while the teacher read the correct answers. Following each chapter, students were tested by means of an objective test which consisted of matching, multiple choice, and fill-in-the-blank statements. All teachers in the department used the same test which was duplicated by the department chairman and distributed to the teachers a few days before the test was to be given. All worksheets and tests were collected at the end of each grading period and destroyed because the same papers were used year after year. I actually tried the system for a few weeks, but I must admit that I felt guilty about the amount of time students spent working quietly, mainly because I missed the daily interaction with my students. I wasn't really teaching and the students weren't really learning. Therefore, I set out to do my own thing. First, each chapter was previewed by discussing the title of the chapter and looking over the subheadings. Pictures were discussed and their captions read. Prior to the actual reading of the chapter, vocabulary words were listed on the board and discussed. Students were asked to give their definitions before referring to the glossary. Where possible, root words and affixes were used to determine word meanings. Parts of chapters were read orally either by students or by me, and instead of doing worksheets, students were taught to outline, a chore they certainly disliked at first, but one in which they all became adept and actually began to enjoy. They were learning to pick out important points on their own and were actually learning. Occasionally, students were divided into groups and given sections of chapters on which to report orally. Departmentalized tests were discarded and replaced with tests which required thinking beyond the purely literal level. There were a few objective questions, but there were also discussion and short answer questions. In addition, there was usually one question on each test which required that students do some creative thinking. For example, on one test students were asked to pretend that they were survivors of an Indian attack on a particular Spanish mission and write a letter to a priest in another mission describing the attack and its results. The students enjoyed writing these letters as much as I enjoyed reading them.

Creativity should not be limited to the English class and compositions. Creative writing assignments in history can help in making history come alive to students. For example, students can project themselves into the past and look at events as they were happening at the time. This can be done in the form of eye-witness accounts or diary or journal entries. A student might pretend he is living in a particular year and write to a friend or relative about current events or life in general in his city, state, or country. Such assignments teach students to look at history from a different perspective and add new meaning to its study.

Of course, there will be students who do not possess the necessary reading ability to handle the material in the social studies text. The teacher should be aware of who these students are by reviewing students' scores on standardized reading tests, which can usually be found in the permanent record folders in the counselor's office. In some schools, students are given reading tests at the beginning of each year in their language arts, English, or reading classes, so current scores may be available from these teachers. It is a good idea to write each student's percentile or grade equivalent score next to that student's name in the grade book so it can be referred to easily. There are several things the teacher can do for those students who may have difficulties with the reading material. Parts of chapters can be read aloud either by the teacher or other students, or chapters can be taped so that poorer readers can follow along as the chapter is read. Good readers will enjoy taking home a blank tape and recording all or part of a chapter for other students to use. Tapes can be reused from year to year so that eventually the entire text is on tape. Class discussion is particularly important for the poor reader because much of what he learns is often oral in nature. Visual aids such as charts, pictures, film strips, and maps also provide another avenue of learning. Group work is important, too, because students can learn from one another. The teacher must not overlook any opportunity for making history a really meaningful learning experience, particularly for the student with reading difficulties.

The library must not be overlooked as a valuable tool for enriching the social studies class. As the teacher covers each new area in the text, he can bring in several books from the school library which provide further information on the subject. During the first few weeks of school, students should be taken to the school library and shown various areas where books, magazines, or reference materials can be found which relate to their text. In addition, classes should be scheduled periodically for the library for research, reports, and free reading in the area of social studies. It should be emphasized that book reports are just as important in social studies as in English class and are generally more meaningful in social studies because they relate to something the students are studying and add to their knowledge of the course.

Lastly, the social studies classroom should be a colorful and inviting place for students, a place with maps, posters, pictures, and books which pertain to areas they are or will be studying. This does not mean, however, that there will be added expense for the social studies teacher. Teachers, as well as students, may be surprised to find that the chambers of commerce in almost any United States city will gladly send free information on their cities just for the asking. Students are thrilled when they actually receive responses from another city or state. Travel magazines contain ads which offer free brochures and information on a multitude of places. Local travel agencies may also be of assistance. Groups of students can be responsible for gathering information and planning bulletin boards on particular areas. Brochures and pamphlets can then be filed for the next year's classes.

As one can see, social studies offers many, many opportunities for meaningful learning experiences. It is an exciting subject that can come alive to students, but only if the teacher becomes actively involved in looking for new and different ways for students to learn. It should not be a dull, boring subject consisting of reading assignments, worksheets, and tests. Like the English class, social studies offers opportunities for creative writing assignments, outlining, library work, book reports, and practical application of study skills. However, in the social studies class, these assignments take on new meaning because they actually relate to something that the students are studying in class.

11 Science, A Neglected Opportunity

Science offers a wonderful opportunity for the teacher to really involve the students in meaningful learning experiences. Because science is the study of the world around us, this subject should prove to be an exciting experience for both teacher and student. Unfortunately, this is not always the case. Science is often a neglected area in our schools, particularly at the kindergarten and elementary levels. In situations where students remain with the same teacher all day, teachers who feel comfortable with science include it in their lesson plans, while others allot little or no time to the subject. Fortunately, some elementary schools do have scheduled science classes as do most middle schools.

Of course, just having science as a part of the curriculum is not enough. Science is a special subject that must be taught in a special way. A science class should include experiences where students are actively involved in the learning process. This means that students must be allowed to work together, they must be allowed to discuss, and they must be allowed to move about the room. This situation may make some teachers nervous and, indeed, some principals, too. There are teachers and principals who feel that learning only takes place in a quiet classroom where students are busily working at their seats. Those educators who feel this way are doing their students a great injustice, for they are depriving their students of valuable learning experiences. Reading a chapter and answering questions day after day is not learning; it is drudgery. Students need to be involved in the learning process. They need to discover and discuss, and above all, they need to learn to think for themselves. Science offers such opportunities, but only if the teacher conducts the class in a meaningful way.

During the course of my graduate studies, I was required, as a part of an elementary science methods class, to teach a fifth-grade science class at a local elementary school one hour a week for eight weeks. To my surprise, the students were not familiar with the scientific method, nor were they allowed to work in groups or conduct their own experiments. If there were demonstrations or experiments to be done, the teacher conducted them while the students observed from their seats. Besides an occasional experiment, the students' days were generally spent reading silently and answering questions in their texts.

My first day with my new students was devoted to talking about science in general and such terms as biology, zoology, botany, and astronomy. We scanned the table of contents in the fifth-grade text and briefly discussed areas they would be studying during the year. We talked about scientists and their work. What does a scientist do? Where does he work? How does he go about solving a problem? My aim, of course, was to lead the students into a discussion of the scientific method and conduct a simple experiment illustrating the use of this valuable learning experience. To familiarize students with the steps in the scientific method, they were each given a sample experiment sheet where they had to write down the problem to be solved, the hypothesis, the procedure used, the data collected, and the conclusion. Each of these areas was thoroughly discussed so that students fully understood the process. Later students would have the opportunity to go through the process on their own.

Meaningful learning takes place only when students get involved in the learning process. For example, reading about magnets and how they work is not a meaningful learning experience. Students must work with real magnets, experiment with them, and discuss what they have learned with their fellow students. Many teachers insist on carrying out all experiments themselves while the class observes. In some instances this might be necessary, but, where possible, students should be allowed to work in small groups with their own supplies. Teachers often complain that group work only results in noise and confusion with little, if anything, being accomplished. In order for group work to be worthwhile, the teacher must lay the groundwork conducive to an atmosphere of learning. First, he must select the students for each group. All groups should be generally equal in overall ability, with each group having both strong and weak students. By organizing groups in this manner, weak students can profit from stronger students' examples.

After groups are set up, each person in the group must be assigned a specific job. Based on a group of five students, one student in each group should be responsible for getting supplies for his table, while another student should be responsible for cleaning up and putting supplies away. One group member should carry out the actual experiment, while another has the responsibility of recording the procedure, the data collected, and the conclusion. Each group should also have someone who is in charge of policing the group and maintaining as much quiet as possible. In groups of less than five students, a student might have two duties to perform. Of course, duties should be rotated so that all students have opportunities to perform all duties.

Group work should become a normal procedure in the science

classroom, not just an occasional divergence for the students. Successful group work actually takes practice in order for things to run smoothly in the classroom. The teacher who tries it one time and gives up frustrated is not giving this procedure a chance and is missing out on a truly rewarding learning experience. When the procedure begins to work, the teacher will see that all his efforts were worthwhile. Students will be learning on their own, they will be excited about their findings, and even the weak students will experience success.

Of course, not every minute of a science class is used to conduct experiments. Reading is an essential part of any science class, but reading from the science text may pose problems for those students who are weak in reading skills. The science teacher must be aware of the reading abilities of her students so that she can anticipate any difficulties they might have. There are too many teachers who simply make a reading assignment and assume that students will have no difficulties with the material.

The technical vocabulary encountered in the science text is a major source of difficulty for many students. Using context to figure out word meanings is of little use in the science class, so students must know the definitions in order to understand the material. Having students define words after a chapter has been read is of little value, but it is a common practice among teachers of every subject. Students need to know the meanings beforehand so they can understand what they are going to read, but even having the students define the words beforehand does not always insure that students understand the meanings. It is important that teachers take the time to go over the pronunciations and meanings of words with the students. Vocabulary study is not an area restricted to the English class. The study of prefixes, suffixes, and root words facilitates the learning of vocabulary in any class. Science vocabulary, in particular, abounds with affixes and root words which appear over and over in the reading material. Students are often required to memorize long lists of these word parts in English class, but it is in science where roots such as micro-, bio-, geo-, astro-, and tele- become truly meaningful. A student who has a basic knowledge of root words and affixes found in many scientific terms soon learns to figure out meanings of words on his own when he encounters them in his reading. Perhaps it would be of benefit to students if the science teacher posted a large chart containing root words and affixes commonly found in their science vocabulary.

In addition to discussing vocabulary, there are a variety of ways in which the teacher can help students handle material in the science text. If students are to read the chapter on their own, the teacher can quickly survey the chapter with students by going over subheadings and reading the captions under pictures or illustrations. He can also set a purpose for reading the material. This can be accomplished in various ways. Of course, students can always be directed to the questions at the end of the chapter before they begin reading, or, by writing two or three questions on the board, the teacher can give the students an idea of what information they should look for while they are reading. Using the SQ3R method, students can also learn to convert bold headings into questions and use these to guide them in picking out important points in their reading. Outlining can also prove useful. The teacher can prepare a simple outline and leave out sections for students to fill in, or students can be taught to prepare their own outlines. The important thing is that students must be given some direction in their reading if the reading assignment is to be meaningful. Assigning ten or twenty pages as homework to be read by the next day's class is generally a waste of time. True, most of the students will probably read the assignment, but will they simply read the words or will they read for meaning? Will they remember one or two disconnected facts or will they come away from the assignment with a general knowledge of what the author had to say? Of course, this will depend on how the teacher prepared the students for the assignment Teachers will find that those five or ten minutes used to preview the chapter greatly determine whether or not students benefit from reading assignments.

It is the teacher's responsibility to set the stage for learning in every class, but it is of particular importance in the science class. Science should not be a class where the teacher does the talking and the students do the listening. Neither should it be a class where students learn solely from reading, answering questions, and doing worksheets. The science class should involve learning experiences designed to not only develop students' thinking abilities and improve their reading skills but to promote responsibility, cooperation with others, and, above all, a good self-concept as they develop confidence in their ability to solve problems. All of this is possible if science is taught in a meaningful way.

12 Testing Must Be Meaningful, Too

Thus far I have attempted to describe ways in which teaching can be made more effective through meaningful learning experiences. However, such experiences serve little purpose if the resultant learning is evaluated by means of a poorly designed test. The written examination is generally the major means of student evaluation, particularly at the secondary level. Because testing does play such an important part in determining students' grades, test construction deserves more attention than it normally receives. We, as teachers, can all recall times when we, as students, felt extremely confident about an upcoming examination, discovering, however, to our bewilderment, that the test covered subject matter which was hardly touched upon in class rather than content the teacher had stressed. Such experiences do little for developing a student's self-confidence. In addition, students soon learn to distrust their teachers and subsequently develop a negative attitude toward the particular subject involved. I suggest that teachers examine their testing methods and strive to make testing, as well as learning, a meaningful part of the classroom experience.

If a test is to be a meaningful experience, it must be carefully thought out and planned by the teacher. I have really never understood how a teacher can spend several weeks on a particular subject or concept and then culminate the learning experience with a test that is made out at the last minute with little or no forethought involved. Indeed, tests are often made out the night before the actual testing and then hurriedly duplicated before class the next day. In fact, tests are often still damp with duplicator fluid when they reach the students' hands. Tests which are typed and duplicated with little or no proofreading usually result in a multitude of questions from students before and during the test. Handwritten tests, as well as tests prepared from last year's faded stencil, are often difficult to read. Teachers who present students with tests such as those described are doing their students an injustice. Tests which are not proofread or are illegible not only result in distracting questions during the testing process but often cause students to make unnecessary errors.

Above all, the testing procedure should be fair. Tests should not be a surprise, nor should the teacher set out to confuse students with trick questions. Students not only should be given ample warning as to the date of the test, but students also should be reviewed and given some idea as to what types of questions will be asked. Will there be mainly essay questions? Will there be multiple choice, fill-in-the-blank, or short answer questions? Approximately how long will the test take? Of course, such information is unavailable if the teacher has yet to make up the test. Teachers will find that students are more relaxed and confident when they know that the test has already been prepared and that they are being reviewed from the actual test.

The idea of fairness also extends to the day of testing. Ample time should be provided for passing out tests and going over test directions and any necessary corrections. Sufficient time should also be allotted for completing the test, as well as providing students the opportunity to double-check their answers. In addition, distractions should be kept to a minimum, so students should not be moving about the room, talking, or engaging in other activities.

A test should be treated as a work of art. It should involve forethought and careful planning. It must be designed not only to measure the abilities of the students but also to adequately test the material which has been covered in class. Last year's test over the same material will not suffice. Not only do teachers present subject matter in different ways from year to year, but also with each new school year come students with different personalities, abilities, and needs. Tests must be designed with this year's students in mind.

Tests are generally looked upon as something separate from the learning process. Though they are mainly designed to measure learning that has already taken place, tests can also serve as a learning tool. By skillfully constructing a test, the teacher can reinforce learning by subtly providing answers to some test questions within other test questions. For example, an answer to a multiple choice question might be revealed with a fill-in-the-blank statement. Information found in objective questions can be used to formulate answers to essay questions. Test directions may even contain information which may be helpful. I am not advocating that teachers make tests too easy, but this type of test construction does teach students to read directions and questions more carefully, particularly if they are made aware that the tests are designed in this manner.

Of course, tests should be challenging, but why not make them interesting as well? If possible, add some humor to the questions. For example, a few ridiculous answers can be included in the multiple choice questions or students' names can be used where possible. In addition to making the test interesting, the humor seems to relax the students. Teachers will find that students actually enjoy tests when this approach is used. It's certainly rewarding to see students smiling or hear them chuckling while taking a test. They know, too, that you have put forth a little extra effort just for them. Matching questions can be made more interesting by having the students unscramble the letters to the answers to form a particular word. It is important, too, that tests contain a variety of question types, not just matching or multiple choice. As early as fifth or sixth grade, teachers can begin including short essay questions on tests to acquaint students with this form of testing. Unfortunately, teachers at all grade levels often avoid such questions because of the time involved in grading anything other than objective type questions. Again, teachers are doing their students an injustice because they are not requiring students to think on any level except a purely literal one. Essay questions teach students to synthesize, analyze, apply, and evaluate what they have learned. Because this area of questioning is often neglected in the school, students entering college are unprepared for essay examinations.

In the first chapter I stated that my frustrations with my daughter's teachers had led me to write this book. A major source of this frustration has been the type of tests administered by the teachers this school year. Several of her teachers insist on giving all major tests orally. As questions are called out, students write down the answers. This, of course, provides no opportunity for them to go back and check or correct answers. When papers are graded and returned, there are only words or letters on the paper so corrections are of little value. This type of testing is fine for daily quizzes where few questions are involved but not for tests which count as a major portion of a student's grade.

Thus far I have described what I believe are the characteristics of a good test. However, any test, no matter how well-planned, soon loses its meaning if not promptly graded and returned to students. Even telling students their grades without letting them see their mistakes contributes nothing to the learning process. Students need to see their mistakes while the material is still fresh in their minds. In fact, class time should be set aside specifically for going over the test and having students make the necessary corrections. This is particularly important in math and English classes where the acquisition of new concepts and skills is dependent on previous learning.

As one can see, the testing procedure should not be taken lightly. If we are to place such importance on the results of testing, then more care must be taken in devising the testing instrument. After all, we do not accept sloppy work from our students, so why do we force them to accept the same from us?

13 Creating an Atmosphere for Meaningful Learning

This book has presented many worthwhile ideas for meaningful learning experiences, but ideas are of little value if the teacher does not create an atmosphere in which meaningful learning can take place. The most important aspect of this atmosphere is the attitude with which both teacher and student approach the learning situation. It is of utmost importance that the teacher approach the school day with a positive attitude. He or she must not bring domestic problems or worries to school but must forget them upon entering the classroom door. Too many teachers vent their frustrations on students by snapping at them, punishing them for small things which ordinarily wouldn't be noticed, and generally making students miserable because of something that is not school-related. There will be days when a teacher must actually pretend that he is enthusiastic about what he is doing even though there are other things on his mind. The teacher must not forget that he has a job to do, a job that demands a positive attitude if meaningful learning is to take place.

Just as important as teacher attitude is student attitude.

Student attitudes toward a particular class are often determined at the classroom door. Is the teacher there waiting to greet students, or is she down the hall talking to another teacher? Or, is she busy at her desk, never bothering to look up until the final bell rings? Does she have a kind word for those who may need some cheering up? Does she compliment those students who may look especially nice that day? These things may seem insignificant, but they are important to the students. In fact, a student's entire day may be changed for the better by a single positive comment by a caring teacher. What happens during those five minutes before class actually begins will greatly determine the extent of learning that day.

A relaxed atmosphere is essential for maximum learning to take place. Students who feel intimidated by the teacher are often reluctant to participate in class discussion or ask questions when they do not understand a particular subject. Moreover, a teacher can easily create tension in the classroom simply by the tone of her voice. Sarcasm and ridicule serve little purpose in the classroom, and, of course, there is definitely something wrong in a classroom where a teacher screams or yells at her students. In fact, I once taught across the hall from a teacher who not only did more screaming than teaching, but she also constantly derided her students and embarrassed them in front of others. Then she wondered why her students did so poorly in her class. They certainly weren't getting any positive support from their teacher, and, if she thought she was helping the students by frightening them into learning, she was sadly mistaken. It's absurd to think that students might benefit from this type of teaching situation; yet, there is at least one teacher like this in every school. A relaxed atmosphere should be one in which students feel comfortable and at ease. They respect the teacher but do not fear him.

Another key factor in creating an atmosphere for learning is classroom organization. Students not only need but want organization in their lives, but students can't be organized unless the teacher is organized. This means that the teacher must know exactly what she will be doing from day to day and week to week. In most classrooms, students get no sense of continuity about the subject because they only know what they are doing at the moment. They do not know how what they are learning today fits into the overall picture. This may not be important to younger elementary students, but by fourth grade, students may begin questioning the necessity of learning a particular subject area and need to have some sense of purpose in what they are doing. In fact, at the beginning of each new school year, teachers need to briefly discuss with the students the areas they will be studying that year. Then, at the beginning of each grading period, they might give students a general outline of specific course material that will be covered during that time period. At the beginning of each week, teachers can briefly discuss what the agenda will be for the week. What pages will be covered that week? Will students need any special materials? Will there be a test scheduled for that week? Will any major assignments be due? It is further suggested that an area of the chalkboard be reserved for such information so students can refer to it when needed. This procedure not only gives students a sense of direction in their studies but also helps to develop confidence in themselves and the teacher.

As for daily organization, an excellent way to begin each class is to have that day's agenda written on the chalkboard so students know what they will be doing during that class. After students are in the classroom, they do not have to wait for instructions from the teacher. They can get out the necessary books and materials without the teacher having to tell them. In fact, it is a good idea to have a short ten-minute assignment for students to begin working on while the teacher checks roll, signs absentee slips, and takes care of any other necessary business. These short assignments can be as simple as answering two or three questions from the text, reading a few pages, defining two or three words, or, in the case of language arts, writing in a journal. These could even be "fun" assignments such as mimeographed puzzles related to that class or trivia questions whose answers are found somewhere in the text. Whatever the assignment, this procedure brings the class to order and helps establish an atmosphere in which learning can take place.

I have purposely left the subject of classroom discipline till last. Naturally, little learning takes place in a classroom where students are noisy, and the teacher is unable to maintain control. Discipline, however, seems to take care of itself when the teacher has created an atmosphere conducive to learning, an atmosphere in which students are relaxed and are not intimidated by the teacher, an atmosphere in which students not only respect the teacher, but also the teacher respects the students. Students with a positive attitude toward both learning and the teacher generally have little reason to create problems because they feel good about themselves and school in general.